DATE DUE AUG 2012

597
Sex   Sexton, Colleen A.
             The life cycle of a sea horse

FOREST PARK PUBLIC LIBRARY

THE LIFE CYCLE OF A
Sea Horse

By Colleen Sexton

Note to Librarians, Teachers, and Parents:

Blastoff! Readers are carefully developed by literacy experts and combine standards-based content with developmentally appropriate text.

Level 1 provides the most support through repetition of high-frequency words, light text, predictable sentence patterns, and strong visual support.

Level 2 offers early readers a bit more challenge through varied simple sentences, increased text load, and less repetition of high-frequency words.

Level 3 advances early-fluent readers toward fluency through increased text and concept load, less reliance on visuals, longer sentences, and more literary language.

Level 4 builds reading stamina by providing more text per page, increased use of punctuation, greater variation in sentence patterns, and increasingly challenging vocabulary.

Level 5 encourages children to move from "learning to read" to "reading to learn" by providing even more text, varied writing styles, and less familiar topics.

Whichever book is right for your reader, Blastoff! Readers are the perfect books to build confidence and encourage a love of reading that will last a lifetime!

This edition first published in 2010 by Bellwether Media, Inc.

No part of this publication may be reproduced in whole or in part without written permission of the publisher. For information regarding permission, write to Bellwether Media, Inc., Attention: Permissions Department, 5357 Penn Avenue South, Minneapolis, MN 55419.

Library of Congress Cataloging-in-Publication Data
Sexton, Colleen A., 1967–
  The life cycle of a sea horse / by Colleen Sexton.
   p. cm. – (Blastoff! Readers life cycles)
Includes bibliographical references and index.
Summary: "Developed by literacy experts for students in kindergarten through grade three, this book follows sea horses as they transform from eggs to adults. Through leveled text and related images, young readers will watch these creatures grow through every stage of life"–Provided by publisher.
  ISBN 978-1-60014-312-0 (hardcover : alk. paper)
 1. Sea horses–Life cycles–Juvenile literature. I. Title.
  QL638.S9S37 2010
  597'.6798–dc22
                                            2009037344

Text copyright © 2010 by Bellwether Media, Inc. BLASTOFF! READERS and associated logos are trademarks and/or registered trademarks of Bellwether Media, Inc.

Printed in the United States of America, North Mankato, MN.
010110   1149

Contents

What Are Sea Horses?	4
Courting	9
The Fry Stage	16
The Adult Stage	20
Glossary	22
To Learn More	23
Index	24

Sea horses are small fish that live in warm ocean waters.

Sea horses have fins, a **snout**, and a tail. Male sea horses have a **pouch**.

Sea horses curl their tails around a plant or **coral**. They hold on tight to keep from floating away on ocean **currents**.

Sea horses can change color. They often match their **surroundings**.

Sea horses grow in stages. The stages of a sea horse's **life cycle** are birth, **fry**, and adult.

The life cycle starts when a male begins to **court** a female. If she chooses him as a **mate**, she visits him every morning. They twist their tails together and go for a swim. They turn the same bright color.

One day the sea horses begin to tilt back and forth and twirl around.

The female's belly grows full with eggs during the courting dance. The male's pouch opens.

The female places her eggs in the male's pouch. Now the male's belly is round.

He sways back and forth to settle the eggs. The pouch seals shut.

The eggs inside the pouch grow into baby sea horses. The pouch grows bigger and bigger.

The male sea horse carries the eggs for about four weeks. He finds a safe place to hide when he is ready to give birth.

The male bends his body back and forth. A baby sea horse pops out of the pouch. The male gives birth to as many as 200 baby sea horses!

A baby sea horse is called a fry. It is the size of a grain of rice and looks like a tiny adult.

A fry lives on its own right away. It hooks its tail around the first plant or piece of coral it sees. Sometimes it even holds on to its father!

The fry eats tiny plants and animals called **plankton**. It sucks plankton in through its snout. The fry eats a lot and grows quickly.

The fry becomes an adult when it is about 6 months old. It searches for a mate.

The adults court and have their own fry. These baby sea horses are the start of a new life cycle!

Glossary

coral—the hard skeletons left behind by small tube-shaped animals called corals; the skeletons build up over time to make coral reefs.

court—the way that animals act before they mate; sea horses do a type of dance before they mate.

current—the movement of water in the ocean

fry—a young fish

life cycle—the stages of life of an animal; a life cycle includes being born, growing up, having young, and dying.

mate—the male or female of a pair of animals

plankton—tiny plants and animals that float in the ocean and are food for other animals; plankton cannot be seen with the human eye.

pouch—a pocket of skin at the base of a male sea horse's tail; eggs grow into baby sea horses inside the pouch.

snout—the long front part of an animal's head that makes up the nose and mouth; the sea horse's snout is a long tube.

surroundings—the area around something; sea horses can change their color to match the plants, rocks, and coral around them.

To Learn More

AT THE LIBRARY
Butterworth, Chris. *Sea Horse: The Shyest Fish in the Sea*. Cambridge, Mass.: Candlewick Press, 2006.

Herriges, Ann. *Sea Horses*. Minneapolis, Minn.: Bellwether Media, 2007.

Schaefer, Lola M. *Sea Horses*. Chicago, Ill.: Heinemann Library, 2002.

ON THE WEB
Learning more about life cycles is as easy as 1, 2, 3.

1. Go to www.factsurfer.com.

2. Enter "life cycles" into the search box.

3. Click the "Surf" button and you will see a list of related Web sites.

With factsurfer.com, finding more information is just a click away.

Index

adult, 8, 17, 20, 21
birth, 8, 15, 16
coral, 6, 18
courting, 9, 11, 21
currents, 6
eggs, 11, 12, 13, 14, 15
fins, 5
fry, 8, 17, 18, 19, 20, 21
life cycle, 8, 9, 21
mate, 9, 20
plankton, 19
pouch, 5, 11, 12, 13, 14, 16
snout, 5, 19
surroundings, 7
tail, 5, 6, 9, 18

The images in this book are reproduced through the courtesy of: National Geographic / Getty Images, front cover (birth), pp. 8 (birth), 16; Jane White / Alamy, front cover (fry), pp. 8 (fry), 17; Gail Shumway, front cover (young adult), p. 18; Bill Kennedy, front cover (adult), p. 20; age fotostock, p. 4; Juan Martinez, pp. 5, 12; Jeff Hunter, p. 6; Nat Sumanatemeya / Alamy, p. 7; Comstock, p. 8 (adult); louise murray / Alamy, p. 9; George Grail, pp. 10, 19; Jeffrey N. Jeffords, p. 11; Seapics, p. 13; Mark Conlin / Alamy, pp. 14-15; Stock Connection Distribution / Alamy, p. 21.